D0425823

The Quotable Woman

RUNNING PRESS
PHILADELPHIA, PENNSYLVANIA

Canadian representatives: General Publishing Co., Ltd.,
30 Lesmill Road, Don Mills, Ontario M3B 2T6.

International representatives: Worldwide Media Services, Inc.,
115 East Twenty-third Street, New York, New York 10010.

9   8   7   6   5   4   3   2   1
Digit on the right indicates the number of this printing.

Library of Congress Cataloging in Publication Number 91–52546

ISBN 1–56138–015–6

Cover calligraphy by Judith Barbour Osborne
Cover design by Toby Schmidt
Interior design by Jacqueline Spadaro
Cover photographs provided by The Granger Collection
Cover and interior illustrations by Steven Nau
Typography by Commcor Communications Corporation, Philadelphia, Pennsylvania

This book may be ordered by mail from the publisher.
Please add $2.50 for postage and handling.
But try your bookstore first!
Running Press Book Publishers
125 South Twenty-second Street
Philadelphia, Pennsylvania 19103

Contents

GEORGIA O'KEEFFE

Being A Woman

a woman is the full circle. Within her is the power to create, nurture, and transform. A woman knows that nothing can come to fruition without light. Let us call upon woman's voice and woman's heart to guide us in this age of planetary transformation.

DIANE MARIECHILD

She must not swing her arms as though they were dangling ropes; she must not switch herself this way and that; she must not shout; and she must not, while wearing her bridal veil, smoke a cigarette.

EMILY POST

To be meek, patient, tactful, modest, honorable, brave, is not to be either manly or womanly; it is to be humane.

JANE HARRISON

One is not born a woman, one becomes one.

SIMONE DE BEAUVOIR

When she stopped conforming to the conventional picture of femininity she finally began to enjoy being a woman.

BETTY FRIEDAN

The especial genius of women I believe to be electrical in movement, intuitive in function, spiritual in tendency.

MARGARET FULLER

From birth to age 18 a girl needs good parents. From 18 to 35 she needs good looks. From 35 to 55 she needs a good personality. From 55 on, she needs good cash.

SOPHIE TUCKER

You don't know a woman until you have had a letter from her.

ADA LEVERSON

It would be curious to discover who it is to whom one writes in a diary. Possibly to some mysterious personification of one's own identity.

BEATRICE WEBB

Once you live with the issue of women and the landscape for a while, you find that you cannot separate them from the notions of peace, spirituality, and community. As women we must learn to become leaders in society, not just for our own sake, but for the sake of all people. We must support and protect our kinship with the environment for the generations to come.

CHINA GALLAND

Because of their agelong training in human relations— for that is what feminine intuition really is—women have a special contribution to make to any group enterprise. . .

MARGARET MEAD

I believe that what woman resents is not so much giving herself in pieces as giving herself purposelessly.

ANNE MORROW LINDBERGH

I feel there is something unexplored about woman that only a woman can explore. . .

GEORGIA O'KEEFFE

A woman's life can really be a succession of lives, each revolving around some emotionally compelling situation or challenge, and each marked off by some intense experience.

WALLIS SIMPSON, DUCHESS OF WINDSOR

Woman: the peg on which the wit hangs his jest, the preacher his text, the cynic his grouch and the sinner his justification.

HELEN ROWLAND

It's the good girls who keep the diaries; the bad girls never have the time.

TALLULAH BANKHEAD

In the Primordial Age Woman Was Once the Sun!

RAICHO HIRATSUKA

...Women have been called queens for a long time, but the kingdom given them isn't worth ruling.

LOUISA MAY ALCOTT

Guilt is the price we pay willingly for doing what we are going to do anyway.

ISABELLE HOLLAND

It's all right for a woman to be, above all, human. I am a woman first of all.

ANAÏS NIN

A woman without a man is like a fish without a bicycle.

GLORIA STEINEM

My idea of superwoman is someone who scrubs her own floors.

BETTE MIDLER

Woman's discontent increases in exact proportion to her development.

ELIZABETH CADY STANTON

Show me a woman who doesn't feel guilty and I'll show you a man.

ERICA JONG

I am the woman who holds up the sky.
The rainbow runs through my eyes.
The sun makes a path to my womb.
My thoughts are in the shape of clouds.
But my words are yet to come.

POEM OF THE UTE INDIANS

Women have served all these centuries as looking glasses possessing the magic and delicious power of reflecting the figure of man at twice its natural size.

VIRGINIA WOOLF

a woman can do anything. She can be traditionally feminine and that's all right; she can work, she can stay at home; she can be aggressive, she can be passive; she can be anyway she wants with a man. But whenever there are the kinds of choices there are today, unless you have some solid base, life can be frightening.

BARBARA WALTERS

we need time to dream, time to remember, and time to reach the infinite. Time to be.

GLADYS TABER

$s$he openeth her mouth with wisdom; and in her tongue is the law of kindness.

PROVERBS

To be somebody, a woman does not have to be more like a man, but has to be more of a woman.

DR. SALLY E. SHAYWITZ

Unfortunately, sometimes people don't hear you until you scream.

STEFANIE POWERS

Women are repeatedly accused of taking things personally. I cannot see any other honest way of taking them.

MARYA MANNES

True strength is delicate.

LOUISE NEVELSON

The idea of strictly minding our own business is moldy rubbish. Who could be so selfish?

MYRTIE BARKER

Woman's virtue is man's greatest invention.

CORNELIA OTIS SKINNER

What you eat standing up doesn't count.

BETH BARNES

I am never afraid of what I know.

ANNA SEWELL

 a woman may develop wrinkles and cellulite, lose her waistline, her bustline, her ability to bear a child, even her sense of humor, but none of that implies a loss of her sexuality, her femininity. . . .

BARBARA GORDON

 a woman must have money and a room of her own.

VIRGINIA WOOLF

2

Action, Achievement, and Ambition

All serious daring starts from within.

EUDORA WELTY

The time when you need to do something is when no one else is willing to do it, when people are saying it can't be done.

MARY FRANCES BERRY

Action is the antidote to despair.

JOAN BAEZ

Each person has his own safe place—running, painting, swimming, fishing, weaving, gardening. The activity itself is less important than the act of drawing on your own resources.

BARBARA GORDON

If you think you can, you can. And if you think you can't, you're right.

MARY KAY ASH

One never notices what has been done; one can only see what remains to be done.

MARIE CURIE

*N*o pessimist ever discovered the secrets of the stars, or sailed to an uncharted land, or opened a new heaven to the human spirit.

HELEN KELLER

*W*hen I look into the future, it's so bright it burns my eyes.

OPRAH WINFREY

*I*t is never too late to be what you might have been.

GEORGE ELIOT

*I*f you can do it then why do it?

GERTRUDE STEIN

*L*ife is to be lived. If you have to support yourself, you had bloody well better find some way that is going to be interesting. And you don't do that by sitting around wondering about yourself.

KATHARINE HEPBURN

*T*here's nothing half so real in life as the things you've done. . .inexorably, unalterably *done*.

SARA TEASDALE

I say if it's going to be done, let's do it. Let's not put it in the hands of fate. Let's not put it in the hands of someone who doesn't know me. I know me best. Then take a breath and go ahead.

ANITA BAKER

There have been women in the past far more daring than we would need to be now, who ventured all and gained a little, but survived after all.

GERMAINE GREER

My mother drew a distinction between achievement and success. She said that achievement is the knowledge that you have studied and worked hard and done the best that is in you. Success is being praised by others, and that's nice, too, but not as important or satisfying. Always aim for achievement and forget about success.

HELEN HAYES

It had long since come to my attention that people of accomplishment rarely sat back and let things happen to them. They went out and happened to *things*.

ELINOR SMITH

Idealists. . . foolish enough to throw caution to the winds. . . have advanced mankind and have enriched the world.

EMMA GOLDMAN

Everyone has talent. What is rare is the courage to follow the talent to the dark place where it leads.

ERICA JONG

You don't get to choose how you're going to die. Or when. You can only decide how you're going to live. Now.

JOAN BAEZ

It is better to die on your feet than to live on your knees.

DOLORES IBARRURI

*Y*ou may be disappointed if you fail, but you are doomed if you don't try.

BEVERLY SILLS

I think it's the end of progress if you stand still and think of what you've done in the past. I keep on.

LESLIE CARON

I do want to get rich but I never want to do what there is to do to get rich.

GERTRUDE STEIN

*Y*esterday I dared to struggle. Today I dare to win.

BERNADETTE DEVLIN

One can never consent to creep when one feels an impulse to soar.

HELEN KELLER

...We are taught you must blame your father, your sisters, your brothers, the school, the teachers—you can blame anyone, but never blame yourself. It's never your fault. But it's ALWAYS your fault, because if you wanted to change, you're the one who has got to change. It's as simple as that, isn't it?

KATHARINE HEPBURN

ANNA PAVLOVA

3

Career and Success

Success can make you go one of two ways. It can make you a prima donna, or it can smooth the edges, take away the insecurities, let the nice things come out.

BARBARA WALTERS

The trouble with being in the rat race is that even if you win, you're still a rat.

LILY TOMLIN

*W*ork is something you can count on, a trusted, lifelong friend who never deserts you.

MARGARET BOURKE-WHITE

I do not know anyone who has got to the top without hard work. That is the recipe. It will not always get you to the top, but should get you pretty near.

MARGARET THATCHER

*N*o one can arrive from being talented alone. God gives talent, work transforms talent into genius.

ANNA PAVLOVA

The fame you earn has a different taste from the fame that is forced upon you.

GLORIA VANDERBILT

To be successful, the first thing to do is fall in love with your work.

SISTER MARY LAURETTA

Success for me is having ten honeydew melons and eating only the top half of each one.

BARBRA STREISAND

KATHERINE MANSFIELD

Self-Esteem

$\mathcal{L}$ove yourself first and everything else falls into line. You really have to love yourself to get anything done in this world.

LUCILLE BALL

*U*ntil you make peace with who you are, you'll never be content with what you have.

DORIS MORTMAN

*W*hat's terrible is to pretend that the second-rate is first-rate. To pretend that you don't need love when you do; or you like your work when you know quite well you're capable of better.

DORIS LESSING

*W*hen we can begin to take our failures nonseriously, it means we are ceasing to be afraid of them. It is of immense importance to learn to laugh at ourselves.

KATHERINE MANSFIELD

I don't need a man to rectify my existence. The most profound relationship we'll ever have is the one with ourselves.

SHIRLEY MacLAINE

...So many of us define ourselves by what we have, what we wear, what kind of house we live in and what kind of car we drive. . . . If you think of yourself as the woman in the Cartier watch and the Hermes scarf, a house fire will destroy not only your possessions but your self.

LINDA HENLEY

*Wh*enever I dwell for any length of time on my own shortcomings, they gradually begin to seem mild, harmless, rather engaging little things, not at all like the staring defects in other people's characters.

MARGARET HALSEY

If you are all wrapped up in yourself, you are overdressed.

KATE HALVERSON

Don't compromise yourself. You are all you've got.

JANIS JOPLIN

The ultimate lesson all of us have to learn is **unconditional love**, which includes not only others but ourselves as well.

ELISABETH KUBLER-ROSS

Let me listen to me and not to them.

GERTRUDE STEIN

master can tell you what he expects of you. A teacher, though, awakens your own expectations.

PATRICIA NEAL

Character builds slowly, but it can be torn down with incredible swiftness.

FAITH BALDWIN

It is hard to fight an enemy who has outposts in your head.

SALLY KEMPTON

One of the things about equality is not just that you be treated equally to a man, but that you treat yourself equally to the way you treat a man.

MARLO THOMAS

I see no reason to keep silent about my enjoyment of
the sound of my own voice as I work.

MURIEL SPARK

*N*obody can make you feel inferior without
your consent.

ELEANOR ROOSEVELT

*W*e are the hero of our own story.

MARY McCARTHY

*T*hink wrongly, if you please, but in all cases think
for yourself.

DORIS LESSING

*Y*ou never find yourself until you face the truth.

PEARL BAILEY

*S*ainthood is acceptable only in saints.

PAMELA HANSFORD JOHNSON

*L*ife is so constructed, that the event does not, cannot, will not, match the expectation.

CHARLOTTE BRONTË

I have often wished I had time to cultivate modesty.
. . . But I am too busy thinking about myself.

EDITH SITWELL

Courage looks you straight in the eye. She is not impressed with power trippers, and she knows first aid. Courage is not afraid to weep, and she is not afraid to pray, even when she is not sure who she is praying to. When she walks it is clear she has made the journey from loneliness to solitude. The people who told me she was stern were not lying; they just forgot to mention she was kind.

J. RUTH GENDLER

I hoped that the trip would be the best of all journeys: a journey into ourselves.

SHIRLEY MacLAINE

I was raised to sense what someone wanted me to be and be that kind of person. It took me a long time not to judge myself through someone else's eyes.

SALLY FIELD

How many cares one loses when one decides not to be something, but to be someone.

COCO CHANEL

I didn't belong as a kid, and that always bothered me. If only I'd known that one day my differentness would be an asset, then my early life would have been much easier.

BETTE MIDLER

You were once wild here. Don't let them tame you!

ISADORA DUNCAN

COLETTE

5

Love and Relationships

What do we live for, if it is not to make life less difficult for each other?

GEORGE ELIOT

Oh, life is a glorious cycle of song, A medley of extemporanea; And love is a thing that can never go wrong; And I am Marie of Roumania.

DOROTHY PARKER

*L*ove never dies of starvation, but often of indigestion.

ANNE DE LENCLOS

*Y*ou can remember the second and the third and the fourth time, but there's no time like the first. It's always there.

SHELAGH DELANEY

*I*f only one could tell true love from false love as one can tell mushrooms from toadstools.

KATHERINE MANSFIELD

*T*o love deeply in one direction makes us more loving in all others.

MADAME SWETCHINE

Love involves a peculiar unfathomable combination of understanding and misunderstanding.

DIANE ARBUS

The more I wonder. . .the more I love.

ALICE WALKER

The Eskimo has fifty-two names for snow because it is important to them; there ought to be as many for love.

MARGARET ATWOOD

The story of a love is not important—what is important is that one is capable of love. It is perhaps the only glimpse we are permitted of eternity.

HELEN HAYES

Trouble is a part of your life, and if you don't share it, you don't give the person who loves you enough chance to love you enough.

DINAH SHORE

Relationship is a pervading and changing mystery. . . brutal or lovely, the mystery waits for people wherever they go, whatever extreme they run to.

EUDORA WELTY

What is important to a relationship is a harmony of emotional roles and not too great a disparity in the general level of intelligence.

MIRRA KOMAROVSKY

...*I* was at a party feeling very shy because there were a lot of celebrities around, and I was sitting in a corner alone and a very beautiful young man came up to me and offered me some salted peanuts and he said, "I wish they were emeralds" as he handed me the peanuts and that was the end of my heart. I never got it back.

HELEN HAYES

*F*or a certain type of woman who risks losing her identity in a man, there are all those questions...until you get to the point and know that you really are living a love story.

ANOUK AIMÉE

*N*o partner in a love relationship...should feel that he has to give up an essential part of himself to make it viable.

MAY SARTON

To love is to receive a glimpse of heaven.

KAREN SUNDE

Do we really know anybody? Who does not wear one face to hide another?

FRANCES MARION

The giving of love is an education in itself.

ELEANOR ROOSEVELT

In real love you want the other person's good. In romantic love you want the other person.

MARGARET ANDERSON

*A*nyone who's a great kisser I'm always interested in.

CHER

*K*nowing is the most profound kind of love, giving someone the gift of knowledge about yourself.

MARSHA NORMAN

...*B*ut surely for everything you love you have to pay some price.

AGATHA CHRISTIE

*N*o temptation can ever be measured by the value of its object.

COLETTE

There are two sorts of romantics: those who love, and those who love the adventure of loving.

LESLEY BLANCH

Love ceases to be a pleasure when it ceases to be a secret.

APHRA BEHN

Love, like a chicken salad or restaurant hash, must be taken with blind faith or it loses its flavor.

HELEN ROWLAND

Joy is a net of love by which you can catch souls.

MOTHER TERESA

*I*f love is the answer, could you please rephrase
the question?

LILY TOMLIN

*T*ears may be dried up, but the heart—never.

MARGUERITE DE VALOIS

A woman has got to love a bad man once or twice in
her life, to be thankful for a good one.

MARJORIE KINNAN RAWLINGS

*W*e can only learn to love by loving.

IRIS MURDOCH

We don't believe in rheumatism and true love until after the first attack.

MARIE VON EBNER-ESCHENBACH

Love is not enough. It must be the foundation, the cornerstone—but not the complete structure. It is much too pliable, too yielding.

BETTE DAVIS

Love is like a violin. The music may stop now and then, but the strings remain forever.

JUNE MASTERS BACHER

There is only one happiness in life, to love and be loved.

GEORGE SAND

There is always something left to love. And if you ain't learned that, you ain't learned nothing.

LORRAINE HANSBERRY

...When we describe what the other person is really like, I suppose we often picture what we want. We look through the prism of our need.

ELLEN GOODMAN

When two people love each other, they don't look at each other, they look in the same direction.

GINGER ROGERS

Love is a game that two can play and both win.

EVA GABOR

*I*deally, couples need three lives; one for him, one for her, and one for them together.

JACQUELINE BISSET

*L*ove's a disease. But curable.

ROSE MACAULAY

*T*he best and most beautiful things in the world cannot be seen or even touched. They must be felt with the heart.

HELEN KELLER

*L*ook for a sweet person. Forget rich.

ESTÉE LAUDER

One of the oldest human needs is having someone to wonder where you are when you don't come home at night.

MARGARET MEAD

True feeling justifies whatever it may cost.

MAY SARTON

Remember my unalterable maxim, "When we love, we always have something to say."

LADY MARY WORTLEY MONTAGU

A caress is better than a career.

ELISABETH MARBURY

We measure success and depth by length of time, but it is possible to have a deep relationship that doesn't always stay the same.

BARBARA HERSHEY

The pain of love is the pain of being alive. It's a perpetual wound.

MAUREEN DUFFY

Age does not protect you from love. But love, to some extent, protects you from age.

JEANNE MOREAU

The only abnormality is the incapacity to love.

ANAÏS NIN

...Love from one being to another can only be that two solitudes come nearer, recognize and protect and comfort each other.

HAN SUYIN (MRS. ELIZABETH COMBER)

Give me a dozen such heartbreaks, if that would help me lose a couple of pounds.

COLETTE

...No one knows how it is that with one glance a boy can break through into a girl's heart.

NANCY THAYER

Boyfriends weren't friends at all; they were prizes, escorts, symbols of achievement, fascinating strangers, the Other.

SUSAN ALLEN TOTH

*L*ove is a fire. But whether it is going to warm your hearth or burn down your house, you can never tell.

JOAN CRAWFORD

I think patience is what love is," he said, "because how could you love somebody without it?"

JANE HOWARD

I don't need an overpowering, powerful, rich man to feel secure. I'd much rather have a man who is there for me, who really loves me, who is growing, who is real.

BIANCA JAGGER

I prefer to explore the most intimate moments, the smaller, crystallized details we all hinge our lives on.

RITA DOVE

I like not only to be loved, but to be told I am loved.

GEORGE ELIOT

The average man is more interested in a woman who is interested in him than he is in a woman with beautiful legs.

MARLENE DIETRICH

It is possible that blondes also prefer gentlemen.

MAMIE VAN DOREN

The act of longing for something will always be more intense than the requiting of it.

GAIL GODWIN

She did observe, with some dismay, that far from conquering all, love lazily sidestepped practical problems.

JEAN STAFFORD

Great loves too must be endured.

COCO CHANEL

*W*e cannot really love anybody with whom we never laugh.

AGNES REPPLIER

*E*ach contact with a human being is so rare, so precious, one should preserve it.

ANAÏS NIN

*W*hen a person that one loves is in the world and alive and well...then to miss them is only a new flavor, a salt sharpness in experience.

WINIFRED HOLTBY

*T*he mark of a true crush...is that you fall in love first and grope for reasons afterward.

SHANA ALEXANDER

...It's so much better to desire than to have. The moment of desire is the most extraordinary moment. The moment of desire, when you *know* something is going to happen—that's the most exalting.

ANOUK AIMÉE

One's life has value so long as one attributes value to the life of others, by means of love, friendship, indignation and compassion.

SIMONE DE BEAUVOIR

When I was very young I fell deeply in love...and really believed I would never feel that way again... then nine years later...I did, and much, much more strongly and deeply than before.

ISAK DINESEN

SIMONE SIGNORET

6

Marriage

One advantage of marriage, it seems to me, is that when you fall out of love with him, or he falls out of love with you, it keeps you together until you maybe fall in love again.

JUDITH VIORST

Husbands are like fires. They go out when unattended.

ZSA ZSA GABOR

The trouble with some women is that they get all excited about nothing—and then marry him.

CHER

An archaeologist is the best husband any woman can have: The older she gets, the more interested he is in her.

AGATHA CHRISTIE

Not all women give most of their waking thoughts to pleasing men. Some are married.

EMMA LEE

Whenever you want to marry someone, go have lunch with his ex-wife.

SHELLEY WINTERS

I prefer the word "homemaker" because "housewife" always implies that there may be a wife someplace else.

BELLA ABZUG

I wanted to sleep with him and I didn't know how to do it without getting married. I talked to everybody, my priest, my doctor, and they all said, "Do it. Get married." Now I could punch them in the nose.

JOAN HACKETT

I know some good marriages—marriages where both people are just trying to get through their days by helping each other, being good to each other.

ERICA JONG

...A man should kiss his wife's navel every day.

NELL KIMBALL

It seemed to me that the desire to get married—which, I regret to say, I believe is basic and primal in women—is followed almost immediately by an equally basic and primal urge—which is to be single again.

NORA EPHRON

Marrying a man is like buying something you've been admiring for a long time in a shop window. You may love it when you get it home, but it doesn't always go with everything else.

JEAN KERR

The hardest task in a girl's life is to prove to a man that his intentions are serious.

HELEN ROWLAND

In a successful marriage, there is no such thing as one's way. There is only the way of both, only the bumpy, dusty, difficult, but always mutual path!

PHYLLIS McGINLEY

It is always incomprehensible to a man that a woman should ever refuse an offer of marriage.

JANE AUSTEN

Marriage is not just spiritual communion and passionate embraces; marriage is also three meals a day, sharing the workload and remembering to carry out the trash.

DR. JOYCE BROTHERS

I suppose when they reach a certain age some men are afraid to grow up. It seems the older the men get, the younger their new wives get.

ELIZABETH TAYLOR

*W*hen he is late for dinner and I know he must be either having an affair or lying dead in the street, I always hope he's dead.

JUDITH VIORST

*I*t was so cold I almost got married.

SHELLEY WINTERS

*C*hains do not hold a marriage together. It is threads, hundreds of tiny threads, which sew people together through the years.

SIMONE SIGNORET

HARRIET BEECHER STOWE

7

Family

I got more children than I can rightly take care of, but I ain't got more than I can love.

OSSIE GUFFY

I looked on child rearing not only as a work of love and duty but as a profession that was fully as interesting and challenging as any honorable profession in the world and one that demanded the best that I could bring to it.

ROSE KENNEDY

When you look at your life, the greatest happinesses are family happinesses.

DR. JOYCE BROTHERS

What feeling is so nice as a child's hand in yours? So small, so soft and warm, like a kitten huddling in the shelter of your clasp.

MARJORIE HOLMES

...a babe at the breast is as much pleasure as the bearing is pain.

MARION ZIMMER BRADLEY

I know of no pleasure that quite matches that of seeing your youngster proudly flaunting something you have made.

RUTH GOODE

If you want a baby, have a new one. Don't baby the old one.

JESSAMYN WEST

The only thing that seems eternal and natural in motherhood is ambivalence.

JANE LAZARRE

Any mother could perform the jobs of several air-traffic controllers with ease.

LISA ALTHER

...There's a lot more to being a woman than being a mother, but there's a hell of a lot more to being a mother than most people suspect.

ROSEANNE BARR

a woman who can cope with the terrible twos can cope with anything.

JUDITH CLABES

...a lot of us who came of age in the 1960s are very wary of authority. But you can't be your child's friend, you have to turn into a parent.

WENDY SCHUMAN

Through our children we. . . have a kind of spiritual reprieve.

EDITH F. HUNTER

*Y*ou have to love your children unselfishly. That's hard. But it's the only way.

BARBARA BUSH

*T*here is nothing more thrilling in this world, I think, than having a child that is yours, and yet is mysteriously a stranger.

AGATHA CHRISTIE

*I*f there were no other reasons (though we know there are as many as stars), this alone would be the value of children: the way they remind you of the comfort of simplicity. Their compelling common sense. Their accessibility and their honesty. Their lack of pretense.

ELIZABETH BERG

A mother is not a person to lean on but a person to make leaning unnecessary.

DOROTHY CANFIELD FISHER

There's a time when you have to explain to your children why they're born, and it's a marvelous thing if you know the reason by then.

HAZEL SCOTT

...What do girls do who haven't any mothers to help them through their troubles?

LOUISA MAY ALCOTT

*W*hen you are a mother, you are never really alone in your thoughts. You are connected to your child and to all those who touch your lives. A mother always has to think twice, once for herself and once for her child.

SOPHIA LOREN

*F*amily faces are magic mirrors. Looking at people who belong to us, we see the past, present, and future.

GAIL LUMET BUCKLEY

*I*n the effort to give good and comforting answers to the young questioners whom we love, we very often arrive at good and comforting answers for ourselves.

RUTH GOODE

*S*eeing you sleeping peacefully on your back among your stuffed ducks, bears and basset hounds, would remind me that no matter how good the next day might be, certain moments were gone forever because we could not go backwards in time.

JOAN BAEZ

*M*aking the decision to have a child—it's momentous. It is to decide forever to have your heart go walking around outside your body.

ELIZABETH STONE

*T*o nourish children and raise them against odds is in any time, any place, more valuable than to fix bolts in cars or design nuclear weapons.

MARILYN FRENCH

Once the children were in the house the air became more vivid and more heated; every object in the house grew more alive.

MARY GORDON

Truth, which is important to a scholar, has got to be concrete. And there is nothing more concrete than dealing with babies, burps and bottles, frogs and mud.

JEANE J. KIRKPATRICK

In the sheltered simplicity of the first days after a baby is born, one sees again the magical closed circle. The miraculous sense of two people existing only for each other.

ANNE MORROW LINDBERGH

*M*ost mothers are instinctive philosophers.

HARRIET BEECHER STOWE

*N*ow, as always, the most automated appliance in a household is the mother.

BEVERLY JONES

I'm not a cookie-baking mother. Well, that's not true. I am a cookie-baking mother. I'm exactly a cookie-baking mother, but I'm not a traditional cookie-baking mother.

CHER

*S*ome are kissing mothers and some are scolding mothers, but it is love just the same, and most mothers kiss and scold together.

PEARL S. BUCK

*I*t goes without saying that you should never have more children than you have car windows.

ERMA BOMBECK

*C*hildren are a house's enemy. They don't mean to be— they just can't help it. It's their enthusiasm, their energy, their naturally destructive tendencies.

DELIA EPHRON

*I*s nothing in life ever straight and clear, the way children see it?

ROSIE THOMAS

*E*ven when freshly washed and relieved of all obvious confections, children tend to be sticky.

FRAN LEBOWITZ

Because I am a mother, I am capable of being shocked: as I never was when I was not one.

MARGARET ATWOOD

A mother is neither cocky, nor proud, because she knows the school principal may call at any minute to report that her child had just driven a motorcycle through the gymnasium.

MARY KAY BLAKELY

Only a mother knows a mother's fondness.

LADY MARY WORTLEY MONTAGU

...The race of children possesses magically sagacious powers!

GAIL GODWIN

It is tough. If you just want a wonderful little creature to love, you can get a puppy.

BARBARA WALTERS

A child of one can be taught not to do certain things such as touch a hot stove, turn on the gas, pull lamps off their tables by their cords, or wake mommy before noon.

JOAN RIVERS

No animal is so inexhaustible as an excited infant.

AMY LESLIE

Perhaps we have been misguided into taking too much responsibility from our children, leaving them too little room for discovery.

HELEN HAYES

The real menace in dealing with a five-year-old is that in no time at all you begin to sound like a five-year-old.

JEAN KERR

Children require guidance and sympathy far more than instruction.

ANNE SULLIVAN

Parents of young children should realize that few people, and maybe no one, will find their children as enchanting as they do.

BARBARA WALTERS

Family jokes, though rightly cursed by strangers, are the bond that keeps most families alive.

STELLA BENSON

Ask your child what he wants for dinner only if he's buying.

FRAN LEBOWITZ

COCO CHANEL

8

Friends

...A friend doesn't go on a diet because you are fat. A friend never defends a husband who gets his wife an electric skillet for her birthday. A friend will tell you she saw your old boyfriend—and he's a priest.

ERMA BOMBECK

We challenge one another to be funnier and smarter. . . It's the way friends make love to one another.

ANNIE GOTTLIEB

Only friends will tell you the truths you need to hear to make. . .your life bearable.

FRANCINE DU PLESSIX GRAY

God gave us our relatives; thank God we can choose our friends.

ETHEL WATTS MUMFORD

Good communication is as stimulating as black coffee, and just as hard to sleep after.

ANNE MORROW LINDBERGH

What I cannot love, I overlook. Is that real friendship?

ANAÏS NIN

My friends, there are no friends.

COCO CHANEL

"Stay" is a charming word in a friend's vocabulary.

LOUISA MAY ALCOTT

Oh Dear! how unfortunate I am not to have anyone to weep with!

MADAME DE SÉVIGNÉ

"Unbosom yourself," said Wimsey. "Trouble shared is trouble halved."

DOROTHY SAYERS

One can never speak enough of the virtues, the dangers, the power of shared laughter.

FRANÇOISE SAGAN

Intimacies between women often go backwards, beginning in revelations and ending in small talk.

ELIZABETH BOWEN

There is space within sisterhood for likeness and difference, for the subtle differences that challenge and delight; there is space for disappointment—and surprise.

CHRISTINE DOWNING

To want friendship is a great fault. Friendship ought to be a gratuitous joy, like the joys afforded by art, or life. . .

SIMONE WEIL

It is very easy to forgive others their mistakes; it takes more grit and gumption to forgive them for having witnessed your own.

JESSAMYN WEST

The hardest of all is learning to be a well of affection, and not a fountain, to show them that we love them, not when we feel like it, but when they do.

NAN FAIRBROTHER

As you grow older, you'll find that you enjoy talking to strangers far more than to your friends.

JOY WILLIAMS

I do not want people to be very agreeable, as it saves me the trouble of liking them a great deal.

JANE AUSTEN

...I have learned that to have a good friend is the purest of all God's gifts, for it is a love that has no exchange of payment.

FRANCES FARMER

Trouble is a sieve through which we sift our acquaintances. Those too big to pass through are our friends.

ARLENE FRANCIS

I always felt that the great high privilege, relief and comfort of friendship was that one had to explain nothing.

KATHERINE MANSFIELD

If it's very painful for you to criticize your friends— you're safe in doing it. But if you take the slightest pleasure in it, that's the time to hold your tongue.

ALICE DUER MILLER

...*It* is that my friends have made the story of my life. In a thousand ways they have turned my limitations into beautiful privileges, and enabled me to walk serene and happy in the shadow cast by my deprivation.

HELEN KELLER

87

Four be the things I am wiser to know: Idleness, sorrow, a friend, and a foe.

DOROTHY PARKER

Treat your friends as you do your picture, and place them in their best light.

JENNIE JEROME CHURCHILL

Each friend represents a world in us, a world possibly not born until they arrive, and it is only by this meeting that a new world is born.

ANAÏS NIN

It is the friends you can call up at 4 A.M. that matter.

MARLENE DIETRICH

...*I*f you want to be listened to, you should put in time listening.

MARGE PIERCY

*Y*es'm, old friends is always best, 'less you can catch a new one that's fit to make an old one out of.

SARAH ORNE JEWETT

...*F*riendships aren't perfect and yet they are very precious. For me, not expecting perfection all in one place was a great release.

LETTY COTTIN POGREBIN

...*O*ne is taught by experience to put a premium on those few people who can appreciate you for what you are. . .

GAIL GODWIN

*S*ilences make the real conversations between friends. Not the saying but the never needing to say is what counts.

MARGARET LEE RUNBECK

*M*y true friends have always given me that supreme proof of devotion, a spontaneous aversion for the man I loved.

COLETTE

9

Challenges

𝒲oman must not accept; she must challenge. She must not be awed by that which has been built up around her; she must reverence that woman in her which struggles for expression.

MARGARET SANGER

*W*hen you get into a tight place and everything goes against you, till it seems as though you could not hang on a minute longer, never give up then, for that is just the place and time that the tide will turn.

HARRIET BEECHER STOWE

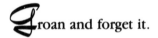roan and forget it.

JESSAMYN WEST

I am not afraid of storms for I am learning how to sail my ship.

LOUISA MAY ALCOTT

*F*or me life is a challenge. And it will be a challenge if I live to be 100 or if I get to be a trillionaire.

BEAH RICHARDS

$\mathcal{I}$ have always grown from my problems and challenges, from the things that don't work out, that's when I've really learned.

CAROL BURNETT

$\mathcal{C}$hallenges make you discover things about yourself that you never really knew. They're what make the instrument stretch—what make you go beyond the norm.

CICELY TYSON

$\mathcal{T}$he healthy and strong individual is the one who asks for help when he needs it. Whether he's got an abscess on his knee or in his soul.

RONA BARRETT

Self-pity in its early stages is as snug as a feather mattress. Only when it hardens does it become uncomfortable.

MAYA ANGELOU

Prejudices, it is well known, are most difficult to eradicate from the heart whose soil has never been loosened or fertilized by education: they grow there, firm as weeds among stones.

CHARLOTTE BRONTË

ISAK DINESEN

10

Happiness

$\mathcal{I}$ don't think that . . . one gets a flash of happiness once, and never again; it is there within you, and it will come as certainly as death . . .

ISAK DINESEN

$\mathcal{E}$arth's crammed with heaven.

ELIZABETH BARRETT BROWNING

A happy woman is one who has no cares at all; a cheerful woman is one who has cares but doesn't let them get her down.

BEVERLY SILLS

Taking joy in life is a woman's best cosmetic.

ROSALIND RUSSELL

The essence of pleasure is spontaneity.

GERMAINE GREER

If you obey all the rules you miss all the fun.

KATHARINE HEPBURN

Today a new sun rises for me; everything lives,
everything is animated, everything seems to speak to me
of my passion, everything invites me to cherish it . . .

ANNE DE LENCLOS

If only we'd stop trying to be happy, we could have a
pretty good time.

EDITH WHARTON

The mere sense of living is joy enough.

EMILY DICKINSON

One must never look for happiness: one meets it by the
way. . . .

ISABELLE EBERHARDT

If you always do what interests you, then at least one person is pleased.

ADVICE TO KATHARINE HEPBURN FROM HER MOTHER

...The greater part of our happiness or misery depends on our dispositions and not on our circumstances.

MARTHA WASHINGTON

Whoever is happy will make others happy too.

ANNE FRANK

Be happy. It's one way of being wise.

COLETTE

The excursion is the same when you go looking for
your sorrow as when you go looking for your joy.

EUDORA WELTY

. . .They seemed to come suddenly upon happiness
as if they had surprised a butterfly in the winter
woods. . .

EDITH WHARTON

...I finally figured out the only reason to be alive is to enjoy it.

RITA MAE BROWN

You have to count on living every single day in a way you believe will make you feel good about your life— so that if it were over tomorrow, you'd be content with yourself.

JANE SEYMOUR

Joy seems to me a step beyond happiness—happiness is a sort of atmosphere you can live in sometimes when you're lucky. Joy is a light that fills you with hope and faith and love.

ADELA ROGERS ST. JOHNS

CLARE BOOTH LUCE

11

Men

$\mathcal{I}$n passing, also, I would like to say that the first time Adam had a chance he laid the blame on woman.

NANCY ASTOR

Personally, I think if a woman hasn't met the right man by the time she's 24, she may be lucky.

DEBORAH KERR

When a man talks to you about his mother's cooking, pay no attention, for between the ages of 12 and 21, a boy can eat large quantities of anything and never feel it.

SARAH TYSON RORER

Plain women know more about men than beautiful ones do.

KATHARINE HEPBURN

Be fond of the man who jests at his scars, if you like; but never believe he is being on the level with you.

PAMELA HANSFORD JOHNSON

$\mathcal{A}$ man's home may seem to be his castle on the outside; inside it is more often his nursery.

CLARE BOOTH LUCE

$\mathcal{W}$hen men talk about defense, they always claim to be protecting women and children, but they never ask the women and children what they think.

PAT SCHROEDER

$\mathcal{N}$o man can be held throughout the day by what happens throughout the night.

SALLY STANFORD

$\mathcal{M}$an forgives woman anything save the wit to outwit him.

MINNA ANTRIM

GEORGE ELIOT

12

The Gender Gap

$\mathcal{S}$ometimes I wonder if men and women really suit each other. Perhaps they should live next door and just visit now and then.

KATHARINE HEPBURN

*W*hen a man gets up to speak, people listen then look. When a woman gets up, people *look*; then, if they like what they see, they listen.

PAULINE FREDERICK

*T*he discovery now being celebrated by men in mid-life of the importance of intimacy, relationships, and care is something that women have known from the beginning. . . . In the different voice of women lies the truth of an ethic of care, the tie between relationship and responsibility, and the origins of aggression in the failure of connection.

CAROL GILLIGAN

*O*ne of my theories is that men love with their eyes; women love with their ears.

ZSA ZSA GABOR

*M*en are taught to apologize for their weaknesses, women for their strengths.

LOIS WYSE

*W*hen a woman behaves like a man, why doesn't she behave like a nice man?

EDITH EVANS

I live by a man's code, designed to fit a man's world, yet at the same time I never forget that a woman's first job is to choose the right shade of lipstick.

CAROLE LOMBARD

A man has to be Joe McCarthy to be called ruthless. All a woman has to do is put you on hold.

MARLO THOMAS

I don't believe man is woman's natural enemy. Perhaps his lawyer is.

SHANA ALEXANDER

After an acquaintance of ten minutes many women will exchange confidences that a man would not reveal to a lifelong friend.

PAGE SMITH

Some of us are becoming the men we wanted to marry.

GLORIA STEINEM

*E*very time we liberate a woman, we liberate a man.

MARGARET MEAD

*I*f only we could all accept that there is no difference between us where human values are concerned. Whatever sex.

LIV ULLMAN

*N*ever go to bed mad. Stay up and fight.

PHYLLIS DILLER

*T*here is more difference within the sexes than between them.

IVY COMPTON-BURNETT

...*I*t seems to me highly improbable that women are going to realize their human potential without alienating men—some men, anyway.

ELIZABETH JANEWAY

*W*hat is most beautiful in virile men is something feminine; what is most beautiful in feminine women is something masculine.

SUSAN SONTAG

I'm not denyin' the women are foolish: God Almighty made 'em to match the men.

GEORGE ELIOT

Thoughts have no sex.

CLARE BOOTH LUCE

There is only one sex.... A man and a woman are so entirely the same thing that one can scarcely understand the subtle reasons for sex distinction with which our minds are filled.

GEORGE SAND

Women want mediocre men, and men are working to be as mediocre as possible.

MARGARET MEAD

𝓘 didn't want to be a boy, ever, but I was outraged that his height and intelligence were graces for him and gaucheries for me.

JANE RULE

𝓣he basic discovery about any people is the discovery of the relationship between men and women.

PEARL S. BUCK

𝓨et if any human being is to reach full maturity both the masculine and feminine sides of the personality must be brought up into consciousness.

M. ESTHER HARDING

MAE WEST

13

Sex

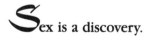 It's not the men in my life, it's the life in my men.

MAE WEST

*S*ex is a discovery.

FANNIE HURST

...You can seduce a man without taking anything off, without even touching him.

RAE DAWN CHONG

It is not sex that gives the pleasure, but the lover.

MARGE PIERCY

I often think that a slightly exposed shoulder emerging from a long satin nightgown packed more sex than two naked bodies in bed.

BETTE DAVIS

I'm suggesting we call sex something else, and it should include everything from kissing to sitting close together.

SHERE HITE

The only sin passion can commit is to be joyless.

DOROTHY SAYERS

Absence does not make the heart grow fonder, but it sure heats up the blood.

ELIZABETH ASHLEY

You mustn't force sex to do the work of love or love to do the work of sex.

MARY McCARTHY

Never underestimate the power of passion.

EVE SAWYER

Too much of a good thing is wonderful.

MAE WEST

In my sex fantasy, nobody ever loves me for my mind.

NORA EPHRON

Sensuality is complicated. Love is intricate. And the
flesh is sweet, but I no longer mistake it for the
whole thing.

CHRIS CHASE

Nothing is either all masculine or all feminine except
having sex.

MARLO THOMAS

How love the limb-loosener sweeps me away. . . .

SAPPHO

We are minor in everything but our passions.

ELIZABETH BOWEN

Shared laughter is erotic too.

MARGE PIERCY

A woman can look both moral and exciting—if she also looks as if it was quite a struggle.

EDNA FERBER

*W*e rarely talk of sex the way men do, in terms of I've had this one, I've had that one. There's a friend I've known for 19 years and all I've known of her private life is what I've heard from others.

JEANNE MOREAU

*N*othing is more revealing than movement.

MARTHA GRAHAM

*T*he act of longing for something will always be more intense than the requiting of it.

GAIL GODWIN

*O*ne should never be sexually involved with anyone one genuinely cares for. A sexual relationship guarantees a loss.

MARY GORDON

All really great lovers are articulate, and verbal seduction is the surest road to actual seduction.

MARYA MANNES

Sex is hardly ever just about sex.

SHIRLEY MacLAINE

I don't think when I make love.

BRIGITTE BARDOT

To err is human—but it feels divine.

MAE WEST

BILLIE HOLIDAY

14

Life Lessons

Arrange whatever pieces come your way.

VIRGINIA WOOLF

How life catches up with us and teaches us to love and forgive each other.

JUDY COLLINS

Someone said that life is a party. You join in after it's started and leave before it's finished.

ELSA MAXWELL

I think the one lesson I have learned is that there is no substitute for paying attention.

DIANE SAWYER

Adventure is something you seek for pleasure, or even for profit, like a gold rush or invading a country; . . . but experience is what really happens to you in the long run; the truth that finally overtakes you.

KATHERINE ANNE PORTER

You can't go around hoping that most people have sterling moral characters. The most you can hope for is that people will pretend that they do.

FRAN LEBOWITZ

People who fight with fire usually end up with ashes.

ABIGAIL VAN BUREN

I like living. I have sometimes been wildly, despairingly, acutely miserable, racked with sorrow, but through it all I still know quite certainly that just to *be alive* is a grand thing.

AGATHA CHRISTIE

You've got to have something to eat and a little love in your life before you can hold still for any damn body's sermon on how to behave.

BILLIE HOLIDAY

Life is easier than you'd think; all that is necessary is to accept the impossible, do without the indispensable, and bear the intolerable.

KATHLEEN NORRIS

One learns in life to keep silent and draw one's own confusions.

CORNELIA OTIS SKINNER

The first problem for all of us, men and women, is not to learn, but to unlearn.

GLORIA STEINEM

The way I see it, if you want the rainbow, you gotta put up with the rain.

DOLLY PARTON

... Life, for all its agonies of despair and loss and guilt, is exciting and beautiful, amusing and artful and endearing, full of liking and love, at times a poem and a high adventure, at times noble and at times very gay; and whatever (if anything) is to come after it—we shall not have this life again.

ROSE MACAULAY

*Y*ou can live a lifetime and, at the end of it, know more about other people than you know about yourself.

BERYL MARKHAM

I began to have an idea of my life, not as the slow shaping of achievement to fit my preconceived purposes, but as the gradual discovery and growth of a purpose which I did not know.

JOANNA FIELD

*M*ake no judgments where you have no compassion.

ANNE McCAFFREY

*A*s time passes we all get better at blazing a trail through the thicket of advice.

MARGOT BENNETT

... As long as one keeps searching, the answers come.

JOAN BAEZ

If you want a place in the sun, you've got to put up with a few blisters.

ABIGAIL VAN BUREN

I have come to the conclusion, after many years of sometimes sad experience, that you cannot come to any conclusion at all.

VITA SACKVILLE-WEST

Time wounds all heels.

JANE ACE

*W*hat you get is a living—what you give is a life.

LILLIAN GISH

I think that wherever your journey takes you, there are new gods waiting there, with divine patience— and laughter.

SUSAN M. WATKINS

*L*ife itself is the proper binge.

JULIA CHILD

*T*he cure for anything is salt water—sweat, tears, or the sea.

ISAK DINESEN

Minor things can become moments of great revelation when encountered for the first time.

MARGOT FONTEYN

Courage is the price that life exacts for granting peace.

AMELIA EARHART

It is best to learn as we go, not go as we have learned.

LESLIE JEANNE SAHLER

Nothing in life is to be feared. It is only to be understood.

MARIE CURIE

*V*itality! That's the pursuit of life, isn't it?

KATHARINE HEPBURN

I might repeat to myself, slowly and soothingly, a list of quotations beautiful from minds profound; if I can remember any of the damn things.

DOROTHY PARKER

*F*ortunately analysis is not the only way to resolve inner conflicts. Life itself still remains a very effective therapist.

KAREN HORNEY

*W*hile others may argue about whether the world ends with a bang or a whimper, I just want to make sure mine doesn't end with a whine.

BARBARA GORDON

Life is the first gift, love is the second, and understanding the third.

MARGE PIERCY

I used to believe that anything was better than nothing. Now I know that sometimes nothing is better.

GLENDA JACKSON

The only interesting answers are those which destroy the questions.

SUSAN SONTAG

Accept the pain, cherish the joys, resolve the regrets; then can come the best of benedictions—"If I had my life to live over, I'd do it all the same."

JOAN McINTOSH

See into life—don't just look at it.

ANNE BAXTER

I have a simple philosophy. Fill what's empty. Empty what's full. And scratch where it itches.

ALICE ROOSEVELT LONGWORTH

The dedicated life is the life worth living. You must give with your whole heart.

ANNIE DILLARD

There are two ways of spreading light: to be the candle or the mirror that reflects it.

EDITH WHARTON

*F*iction reveals truths that reality obscures.

JESSAMYN WEST

... *I* am incapable of conceiving infinity, and yet I do not accept finity. I want this adventure that is the context of my life to go on without end.

SIMONE DE BEAUVOIR

*L*earn the wisdom of compromise, for it is better to bend a little than to break.

JANE WELLS

It had been my repeated experience that when you said to life calmly and firmly (but very firmly!), "I trust you; do what you must," life had an uncanny way of responding to your need.

OLGA ILYIN

If we could sell our experiences for what they cost us we'd be millionaires.

ABIGAIL VAN BUREN

Of two evils choose the prettier.

CAROLYN WELLS

*K*eep your face to the sunshine and you cannot see the shadows.

HELEN KELLER

*N*ever mistake knowledge for wisdom. One helps you make a living; the other helps you make a life.

SANDRA CAREY

*S*tanding in the middle of the road is very dangerous; you get knocked down by traffic from both sides.

MARGARET THATCHER

*N*ever eat more than you can lift.

MISS PIGGY

15

Mistakes

*M*istakes are part of the dues one pays for a full life.

SOPHIA LOREN

*I*f. . .you can't be a good example, then you'll just have to be a horrible warning.

CATHERINE AIRD

It's never too late—in fiction or in life—to revise.

NANCY THAYER

I'll match my flops with anybody's but I wouldn't have missed 'em. Flops are a part of life's menu and I've never been a girl to miss out on any of the courses.

ROSALIND RUSSELL

It is always one's virtues and not one's vices that precipitate one into disaster.

REBECCA WEST

*A*ccept that all of us can be hurt, that all of us can— and surely will at times—fail. Other vulnerabilities, like being embarrassed or risking love, can be terrifying too. I think we should follow a simple rule: if we can take the worst, take the risk.

DR. JOYCE BROTHERS

*I*f you have made mistakes. . .there is always another chance for you. . .you may have a fresh start any moment you choose, for this thing we call "failure" is not the falling down, but the staying down.

MARY PICKFORD

*Y*ou will do foolish things, but do them with enthusiasm.

COLETTE

ANNA FREUD

16

Mind and Body

At every moment, our bodies are continually responding to the messages from our minds. So what messages is your mind giving your body?

MARGO ADAIR

The Rubicons which women must cross, the sex barriers which they must breach, are ultimately those that exist in their own minds.

FREDA ADLER

Above all, remember that the most important thing you can take anywhere is not a Gucci bag or French-cut jeans; it's an open mind.

GAIL RUBIN BERENY

Creative minds have always been known to survive any kind of bad training.

ANNA FREUD

The best mind-altering drug is truth.

LILY TOMLIN

The human mind always makes progress, but it is a progress in spirals.

MADAME DE STAEL

I'm always fascinated by the way memory diffuses fact.

DIANE SAWYER

MARY WOLLSTONECRAFT SHELLEY

17

Beauty

People see you as an object, not as a person, and they project a set of expectations onto you. People who don't have it think beauty is a blessing, but actually it sets you apart.

CANDICE BERGEN

I adore wearing gems, but not because they are mine. You can't possess radiance, you can only admire it.

ELIZABETH TAYLOR

It is hardly surprising that women concentrate on the way they look instead of what was in their minds since not much has been put in their minds to begin with.

MARY WOLLSTONECRAFT SHELLEY

If truth is beauty, how come no one has their hair done in a library?

LILY TOMLIN

I don't think of all the misery, but of all the beauty that still remains.

ANNE FRANK

One cannot collect all the beautiful shells on the beach. One can collect only a few, and they are more beautiful if they are few.

ANNE MORROW LINDBERGH

PEARL BAILEY

18

Time and Change

The moment of change is the only poem.

ADRIENNE RICH

Life forms illogical patterns. It is haphazard and full of beauties which I try to catch as they fly by, for who knows whether any of them will ever return?

MARGOT FONTEYN

Time is a dressmaker specializing in alterations.

FAITH BALDWIN

The only thing that makes life possible is permanent, intolerable uncertainty: not knowing what comes next.

URSULA K. LeGUIN

People change and forget to tell each other.

LILLIAN HELLMAN

...Some things. . .arrive in their own mysterious hour, on their own terms and not yours, to be seized or relinquished forever.

GAIL GODWIN

Memory is more indelible than ink.

ANITA LOOS

Someday perhaps change will occur when times are ready for it instead of always when it is too late. Someday change will be accepted as life itself.

SHIRLEY MacLAINE

The events of childhood do not pass, but repeat themselves like seasons of the year.

ELEANOR FARJEON

I think that one's art is a growth inside one. I do not think one can explain growth. It is silent and subtle. One does not keep digging up a plant to see how it grows.

EMILY CARR

Change is an easy panacea. It takes character to stay in one place and be happy there.

ELIZABETH CLARKE DUNN

Birds sing after a storm; why shouldn't people feel as free to delight in whatever remains to them?

ROSE KENNEDY

I must govern the clock, not be governed by it.

GOLDA MEIR

*I*t seems necessary to completely shed the old skin
before the new, brighter, stronger, more beautiful one can
emerge. . .I never thought I'd be getting a life lesson from
a snake!

JULIE RIDGE

*W*e grow in time to trust the future for our answers.

RUTH BENEDICT

*S*ometimes I would almost rather have people take
away years of my life than take away a moment.

PEARL BAILEY

$\mathcal{E}$verything in life that we really accept undergoes
a change.

KATHERINE MANSFIELD

$\mathcal{L}$iving the past is a dull and lonely business; looking
back strains the neck muscles, causes you to bump into
people not going your way.

EDNA FERBER

$\mathcal{T}$here has never been an age that did not applaud the
past and lament the present.

LILLIAN EICHLER WATSON

That is what learning is. You suddenly understand
something you've understood all your life, but in a
new way.

DORIS LESSING

We are tomorrow's past.

MARY WEBB

I have accepted fear as a part of life—specifically the
fear of change. . .I have gone ahead despite the pounding
in the heart that says: turn back. . .

ERICA JONG

I do not think that I will ever reach a stage when I will say, "This is what I believe. Finished." What I believe is alive. . .and open to growth. . . .

MADELEINE L'ENGLE

To keep our faces toward change and behave like free spirits in the presence of fate is strength undefeatable.

HELEN KELLER

The events in our lives happen in a sequence in time but in their significance to ourselves they find their own order. . .the continuous thread of revelation.

EUDORA WELTY

BETTE DAVIS

19

Age

I'd like to grow very old as slowly as possible.

IRENE MAYER SELZNICK

And then, not expecting it, you become middle-aged and anonymous. No one notices you. You achieve a wonderful freedom. It is a positive thing. You can move about, unnoticed and invisible.

DORIS LESSING

In youth we learn; in age we understand.

MARIE VON EBNER-ESCHENBACH

There is a fountain of youth: it is your mind, your talents, the creativity you bring to your life and the lives of people you love. When you learn to tap this source, you will have truly defeated age.

SOPHIA LOREN

You grow up the day you have your first real laugh at yourself.

ETHEL BARRYMORE

Everything else you grow out of, but you never recover from childhood.

BERYL BAINBRIDGE

*F*ull maturity. . . is achieved by realizing that you have choices to make.

ANGELA BARRON McBRIDE

*I*t is sad to grow old but nice to ripen.

BRIGITTE BARDOT

*N*ature gives you the face you have at twenty; it is up to you to merit the face you have at fifty.

COCO CHANEL

*W*e grow neither better nor worse as we get old, but more like ourselves.

MAY LAMBERTON BECKER

Age is something that doesn't matter, unless you are a cheese.

BILLIE BURKE

One of the many things nobody ever tells you about middle age is that it's such a nice change from being young.

DOROTHY CANFIELD FISHER

We are always the same age inside.

GERTRUDE STEIN

The secret of staying younger is to live honestly, eat slowly, and just not think about your age.

LUCILLE BALL

I've always believed in the adage that the secret of eternal youth is arrested development.

ALICE ROOSEVELT LONGWORTH

After a certain number of years, our faces become our biographies.

CYNTHIA OZICK

I've always roared with laughter when they say life begins at forty. That's the funniest remark ever. The day I was born was when life began for me.

BETTE DAVIS

Time—our youth—it never really goes, does it? It is all held in our minds.

HELEN HOOVER SANTMYER

20

Opportunity

Why not seize the pleasure at once? How often is happiness destroyed by preparation, foolish preparation!

JANE AUSTEN

Luck is a matter of preparation meeting opportunity.

OPRAH WINFREY

The more the years go by, the less I know. But if you give explanations and understand everything, then nothing can happen. What helps me go forward is that I stay receptive, I feel that anything can happen.

ANOUK AIMÉE

Fortunately for children, the uncertainties of the present always give way to the enchanted possibilities of the future.

GELSEY KIRKLAND

But to look back all the time is boring. Excitement lies in tomorrow.

NATALIA MAKAROVA

I make the most of all that comes and the least of all that goes.

SARA TEASDALE

BEVERLY SILLS

21

Power

The thing women have got to learn is that nobody gives you power. You just take it.

ROSEANNE BARR

There is a growing strength in women but it's in the forehead, not the forearm.

BEVERLY SILLS

*U*nless you choose to do great things with it, it makes no difference how much you are rewarded, or how much power you have.

OPRAH WINFREY

*I*t of course makes eminent sense that the earliest depiction of divine power in human form should have been female rather than male. When our ancestors began to ask the eternal question...they must have noted that life emerges from the body of a woman.... It further seems logical that women would not be seen as subservient in societies that conceptualize the powers governing the universe in female form—and the "effeminate" qualities such as caring, compassion and nonviolence would be highly valued in these societies. What does *not* make sense is to conclude that societies in which men did not dominate women were societies in which women dominated men.

RIANNE EISLER

*W*omen have had the power of naming stolen from us.

MARY DALY

*O*nce, power was considered a masculine attribute. In fact, power has no sex.

KATHERINE GRAHAM

*I*f I'm too strong for some people, that's their problem.

GLENDA JACKSON

*P*ower can be seen as power with rather than power over, and it can be used for competence and co-operation, rather than dominance and control.

ANNE L. BARSTOW

SIMONE DE BEAUVOIR

Individuality

*W*hat a sense of superiority it gives one to escape
reading some book which everyone else is reading.

ALICE JAMES

*W*omen and men in the crowd meet and mingle,
Yet with itself every soul standeth single.

ALICE CARY

Constant togetherness is fine—but only for Siamese twins.

VICTORIA BILLINGS

I wish that every human life might be pure transparent freedom.

SIMONE DE BEAUVOIR

It all starts with self-reflection. Then you can know and empathize more profoundly with someone else.

SHIRLEY MacLAINE

Men say they love independence in a woman, but they don't waste a second demolishing it brick by brick.

CANDICE BERGEN

It is easy to be independent when you've got money.
But to be independent when you haven't got a thing—
that's the Lord's test.

MAHALIA JACKSON

I like being unconventional.

FLORENCE GRIFFITH JOYNER

I like a view but I like to sit with my back turned to it.

GERTRUDE STEIN

Respect . . . is appreciation of the **separateness** of the
other person, of the ways in which he or she is unique.

ANNIE GOTTLIEB

*C*herish forever what makes you unique, 'cuz you're really a yawn if it goes!

BETTE MIDLER

*S*olitude is un-American.

ERICA JONG

*W*hat a lovely surprise to discover how un-lonely being alone can be.

ELLEN BURSTYN

*F*ond as we are of our loved ones, there comes at times during their absence an unexplained peace.

ANNE SHAW

MAY SARTON

23

Day-to-Day Living

$\mathcal{E}$ach day, and the living of it, has to be a conscious creation in which discipline and order are relieved with some play and pure foolishness.

MAY SARTON

There is no pleasure in having nothing to do; the fun is in having lots to do and not doing it.

MARY LITTLE

Never get so fascinated by the extraordinary that you forget the ordinary.

MAGDALEN NABB

Cleaning your house while your kids are still growing is like shoveling the walk before it stops snowing.

PHYLLIS DILLER

You don't get over hating to cook, any more than you get over having big feet.

PEG BRACKEN

Don't you think that the best things are already in view?

JULIA WARD HOWE

It seems to me I spent my life in car pools, but you know, that's how I kept track of what was going on.

BARBARA BUSH

The only courage that matters is the kind that gets you from one minute to the next.

MIGNON McLAUGHLIN

Were women meant to do everything—work and have babies?

CANDICE BERGEN

*W*hen something does not insist on being noticed, when we aren't grabbed by the collar or struck on the skull by a presence or an event, we take for granted the very things that most deserve our gratitude.

CYNTHIA OZICK

*I*f a few lustful and erotic reveries make the housework go by "as if in a dream," why not?

NANCY FRIDAY

*M*y husband and I have figured out a really good system about the housework: neither one of us does it.

DOTTIE ARCHIBALD

To have a reason to get up in the morning, it is necessary to possess a guiding principle.

JUDITH GUEST

When you're an orthodox worrier, some days are worse than others.

ERMA BOMBECK

Never economize on luxuries.

ANGELA THIRKELL

24

Words

Kind words can be short and easy to speak, but their echoes are truly endless.

MOTHER TERESA

...**W**ords are a form of action, capable of influencing change. Their articulation represents a complete, lived experience.

INGRID BENGIS

25

Manners

*M*anners are a sensitive awareness of the feelings of others. If you have that awareness, you have good manners, no matter what fork you use.

EMILY POST

Good taste is the worst vice ever invented.

EDITH SITWELL

I've done more harm by the falseness of trying to
please than by the honesty of trying to hurt.

JESSAMYN WEST

The most exhausting thing in life is being insincere.

ANNE MORROW LINDBERGH

26

Spirituality

...It isn't until you come to a spiritual understanding of who you are—not necessarily a religious feeling, but deep down, the spirit within—that you can begin to take control.

OPRAH WINFREY

Spiritual and religious traditions, when shaped by the feminine principle, affirm the cyclical phases of our lives and the wisdom each phase brings, the sacredness of our bodies and the body of the Earth.

PATRICE WYNNE

It's better to have a rich soul than to be rich.

OLGA KORBUT

My deepest impulses are optimistic; an attitude that seems to me as spiritually necessary and proper as it is intellectually suspect.

ELLEN WILLIS

Invest in the human soul. Who knows, it might be a diamond in the rough.

MARY McLEOD BETHUNE

Reach high, for stars lie hidden in your soul. Dream deep, for every dream precedes the goal.

PAMELA VAULL STARR

...Dreams are, by definition, cursed with short life spans.

CANDICE BERGEN

Hope is a very unruly emotion.

GLORIA STEINEM

Dreams have only one owner at a time. That's why dreamers are lonely.

ERMA BOMBECK

Imagination is the highest kite one can fly.

LAUREN BACALL

I was not looking for my dreams to interpret my life, but rather for my life to interpret my dreams.

SUSAN SONTAG

For to dream and then to return to reality only means that our qualms suffer a change of place and significance.

COLETTE

Rose-colored glasses are never made in bifocals. Nobody wants to read the small print in dreams.

ANN LANDERS

Dreams say what they mean, but they don't say it in daytime language.

GAIL GODWIN

The dream was always running ahead of one. To catch up, to live for a moment in unison with it, that was the miracle.

ANAÏS NIN

I believe that dreams transport us through the underside of our days, and that if we wish to become acquainted with the dark side of what we are, the signposts are there, waiting for us to translate them.

GAIL GODWIN

There are many things in your heart you can never tell to another person. They are you, your private joys and sorrows, and you can never tell them. You cheapen them, the inside of yourself when you tell them.

GRETA GARBO

*M*ake-believe colors the past with innocent distortion, and it swirls ahead of us in a thousand ways —in science, in politics, in every bold intention. It is part of our collective lives, entwining our past and our future. . .a particularly rewarding aspect of life itself.

SHIRLEY TEMPLE BLACK

I've dreamt in my life dreams that have stayed with me ever after, and changed my ideas; they've gone through and through me, like wine through water, and altered the color of my mind.

EMILY BRONTË

*I*t seems to me we can never give up longing and wishing while we are alive. There are certain things we feel to be beautiful and good, and we must hunger for them.

GEORGE ELIOT

If you can remember dreams of flying and soaring like a bird, or dancing, or singing more perfectly than you ever thought possible, you know that no second-hand account of such events could ever give you the thrill you felt in the dream.

GAYLE DELANEY

It takes a lot of courage to show your dreams to someone else.

ERMA BOMBECK

If one is lucky, a solitary fantasy can totally transform one million realities.

MAYA ANGELOU

Index